All Families Are
Different

ISBN: 978-1-60169-397-6

Published by innovativeKids®
A division of innovative USA®, Inc.
49 Richmondville Ave.
Westport, CT 06880
iKids is a registered trademark in Canada and Australia.

www.innovativekids.com

Printed in USA
1 3 5 7 9 10 8 6 4 2
First Edition

Today was family day at my school. Everyone got to go up on stage and talk about their families.

I have a mom, a dad, a dog, and two goldfish in my family. I love my family very much.

My dog showed off his best tricks!

He even gave my teacher a big, wet kiss!

I used to think every family had to have a mommy, a daddy and a kid like me.

But today I learned that families are all different.

Families come in all different sizes, shapes, and colors.

Some are big.

Some are small.

And some have
lots of
furry friends!

Some families live in houses . . .

. . . some in apartments . . .

. . . and some even live on farms!

My friend Jane has a very big family. She has a mom, a dad, and eight brothers and sisters.

It must be loud in Jane's house.

My friend Danny was adopted from China, and his brother was adopted from Africa.

Danny and his brother look different from each other. They also look different from their mom and dad.

My friends Jack and Charlie are twins. They look exactly alike. Sometimes our teacher can't even tell them apart.

My friend Sam has a sister and a pet rabbit. Sam's mom is from Mexico and his dad is from Japan. Sam and his sister speak three different languages.

Did you know that some kids don't have both a mom and a dad in their families? My friend Zoe has two dads, and Thomas has two moms.

My friend Ari has just a mom. He had only two people in his family until last weekend, when he got a new kitten.

Ben has a mom and a dad, but they are divorced. Some days he lives with his mom, and other days he lives with his dad.

Sadie lives with her grandma and her three older brothers. Sadie and her brothers do a lot of chores to help their grandma around the house.

I learned a lot about families today.

Families make you laugh when you drop your ice cream cone.

Families snuggle you when you're afraid of the dark.

Families cheer you on when you
reach the finish line.

Families give you piggyback rides
when you're too tired to walk.

Families can look very different
on the outside.

But there is something very special
on the inside that makes all families
the same . . .

. . . and that is LOVE.

A Note to Parents

In today's world, families come in all different shapes, sizes, and colors. Nontraditional families are more common than ever before, and many children live in blended, adoptive, single-parent, or gay and lesbian families.

At two or three years old, children may not question their families or the families around them, but as they grow and interact with peers, that will change. When preschoolers transition to school or other social settings, you can expect them to start asking questions. At this time, it is important for children to know that while families can look very different on the outside, there is a special ingredient called LOVE that holds each and every family together.

Here are a few things to think about when you are talking to your child about how families are different:

☐ Use children's books: This book and other children's books about families are great resources to share with inquisitive youngsters. Carefully selected books can help a child understand the concept of different families in an appropriate and light-hearted way. In addition, children's books can be a gentle way to start a discussion with your child when you yourself aren't sure how to begin.

☐ Keep it simple: Follow your child's cues and answer questions with simple responses rather than going into a long and detailed discussion.

☐ Be positive: Remember to think about the message you want to send to your child. You can help your child feel comfortable by speaking positively about all different types of families.

☐ Model acceptance: You are your child's number one teacher! When your child notices that a family is different, remind him or her that families come in all shapes, sizes, and colors. By modeling acceptance of different families, you will encourage your child to do the same.

☐ Organize playdates: Exposing your child to families that are the same and families that are different from your own is a great way to help your child feel comfortable and gain firsthand exposure to different types of family structures.

☐ Repeat yourself: Remind your child often that it's love that makes a family a family, no matter what combination of people are involved. Reassure your child that a family can be any group of people who love and take care of each other. This repeated message helps them feel secure in their own family structure, even if it were to change.

Just remember, family = love.

My Family Tree

Fill in the spaces on the tree with the names of all the people in your family!

Your name here